HOW TO FEED A HORSE

HOW TO FEED A HORSE

poems

Janice Dewey

 Crooked Hearts Press

You shall love your crooked neighbor
with your crooked heart.

—W. H. Auden

Acknowledgments: "Sound Pillows," "Electricity," and "Moon" appeared in *Spiral Orb*
#6 (2013). "Red Juice" and "Guidebook to the Maladies" appeared in *The Daybreak and
Willingness Club* (4D Productions, 2002).

Library of Congress Cataloging-in-Publication Data

Names: Dewey, Janice, author.
Title: How to feed a horse : poems / Janice Dewey.
Description: First edition. | Pasadena : Crooked Hearts Press, [2021]
Identifiers: LCCN 2020041003 | ISBN 9781597098663 (trade paperback) | ISBN
    9781597098670 (epub)
Subjects: LCGFT: Poetry.
Classification: LCC PS3604.E9165 H69 2021 | DDC 811/.6—dc23
LC record available at https://lccn.loc.gov/2020041003

The National Endowment for the Arts, the Los Angeles County Arts Commission,
the Ahmanson Foundation, the Dwight Stuart Youth Fund, the Max Factor Family
Foundation, the Pasadena Tournament of Roses Foundation, the Pasadena Arts &
Culture Commission and the City of Pasadena Cultural Affairs Division, the City of
Los Angeles Department of Cultural Affairs, the Audrey & Sydney Irmas Charitable
Foundation, the Kinder Morgan Foundation, the Meta & George Rosenberg Founda-
tion, the Albert and Elaine Borchard Foundation, the Adams Family Foundation, the
Riordan Foundation, Amazon Literary Partnership, the Sam Francis Foundation,
and the Mara W. Breech Foundation partially support Red Hen Press.

First Edition
Published by Crooked Hearts Press
an imprint of Red Hen Press
www.redhen.org
www.crookedheartspress.org

Acknowledgments

I would like to acknowledge my writing group first and foremost, for through this community I gained the confidence to write and keep writing: Karen Falkenstrom, Lisa Cooper, Barbara Allen, Barrie Ryan, Rita Magdaleno. Gracias, queridas hermanas.

The Poetry Center at the University of Arizona has been my laboratory, educational fountain of living words, and platform for teaching for over two decades. Through various directors Alison Deming, Mark Wunderlich, Frances Sjoberg, Gail Browne, and Tyler Meier, the center continues its renowned and successful mission. Dean Pat MacCorquodale assured my place there with honors students, where we shared the past, the now, and the future through poetry. I thank you all for this synergy.

I am forever grateful to these exceptional readers/editors: Barbara Allen, Richard Shelton, Barbara Cully, Karen Brennan, and Cynthia Hogue, poets extraordinaire.

I wish to acknowledge my sister, Donna. Our constant conversations and travels through languages and their peoples are as regular as the tides.

Barrie Ryan and Mezcal Mt. Ranch were the beginning of things, and so many poems came out of that riparian paradise. And little did I know when Eleanor Wilner entered my classroom that she would be the propulsion for this book. My deepest gratitude to both, for they are in their own ways the alpha and omega of this project.

For my dearest friend, Barbara Allen, I can only say thank you for helping, supporting, inspiring, and making me laugh. Our friendship has always walked crooked, driven crooked, and talked crooked with love.

Without these angels, no book:

Barrie Mirto Barbara

Cynthia Eleanor

Marcella

Inferno

Summer inferno with drought markers: grasshopper invasion biting flies
gas refrigerator dead   herding dogs exhausted from shooing horned creatures
creek artery drying out

sitting there in the long-looking long field

orange brown dried leaves

stark armed and legged trees

so much hacking by chain now
sycamores and ash

one bird and one bird

looking south toward the Gila snaking water

green soaked treasure grove borders the cattle

arranges them along broken limbs where they twist stalks of seep willow
flourishing in green   brooking the landscape and brooming it too

one bird and one bird in field capsule   hover in want

Contents

NUMEROLOGY

HER(E)

Bull's Eye

In the practice of eternity trees rocket to the surface over eons
fish swim in schools through never-ending
curvaceous waves

the practice of eternity opens doors for the dead
that they may come to supper and blow out candles
(for this is common to calendar time)

but how to hear the voice
the one never recorded
here, now, seated at the table

the so long ago voice, gravelly cinders of tender language not
sounding at ghost dinner

the practice of eternity is wandering amongst the grand appearances barefoot
allows the earth to give under the feet
reminds of volcanic archives bent on opening, charging anytime

for the practice of eternity an archer sucks in breath
counts to five and releases to target

dead on

Ranch Triptych

1. She climbs up the creek

   two tree limbs support two

   legs and arthritic body

   a wince, a homecoming

   She knows she'll make it

   with the heaves and sighs

   heart engine firing sounds

   of effort and possible

   Creek runs toward the Gila

   and washes through watercress

   while she startles forward

   through silt, the murmurs

   water grows a sky

   and dry up ahead

2. Because the mountains have

    handed over the mule deer

    and day's sun

    they are blue

    Because the raven doesn't

    walk today but

    measures by wingbeats

    and senses of rain

    raven throat soaks song

    Because the letters don't mean

    much when you can't see them

    but mean anything

    —a rattle—

    when you hear them connected

    their own kind of fence

3.   Does the one-eyed puma

    know half the story?

    true, the lions take half

    the calf crop

    the Herefords are half

    white   half red

    the Charolais are golden

    one hue

    stock dogs black-and-white

    half-and-half like Holsteins

    bark at heads

    bite at tails

    creek walker, she

    knows half of her has

    gone missing for years now.

Coyote Dog

Coyote Dog didn't need to log onto beliefnet.com to pick stars or spirits of the Day. It was Friday the Playday, one for fools and poised dancers and a steep ledge of recognition to slide down, belly primed with prickly pear and rat.

The other pack howlers were way off and keening, night wind a telephone line straight to Coyote Dog sitting ledge watch on sacred haunches, the nose aloft and ears prickled, giant sound receptors for desert wisdom:

I hear you rustling Colorado Toad. You can't hide those clicks or that plopping girth. Take this message back to creek rocks: one can't move along the sand without an exit strategy, one can't hide in the water without air. Tell the rocks to stay where they are until the pack arrives to lick their quartz faces.

CANYON WREN

Chapter one

Home

Canyon wren has begun another nest inside the ranch house

northeast corner of a window sill

> black and white dog hair

> longer silvery hair of dog owner

> mattress lining   leaves   tiny twigs

all improve the lost art of reading—that wordy network

of pleasure and contemplation

the seeing and the sitting, coming and going arrangement

tending to earth birthdays and then the feeding

with her long bill and mate's falling soprano call

canyon wren flits and dives in and out of the cabin made from

creek trees

through her secret hole under the eaves

she's begun a new novel, a bildungsroman

Chapter two
Canyon Wren Moving, Transfer and Storage

The nest had disappeared   no trace   but found on the floor

the tender center made of dog and human hair

inside the second door the wren flew and flit flew and flit

buzzing with perk

from bathroom to kitchen and out through the ceiling to bright

foliage   and in again to scoot the floors and hop from pan

to pan

the woman sat in meditation at the window

the oriole nest that had hung high as decoration over her seat

had fallen to the floor

fluffy dog hair of Zoe, life magnificent   gorgeous coyote dog

with black eyeliner

was missing inside the woven orb

Chapter three
Sound Pillows

The sky opened at 5:20 with orange pillows

cool breeze on her face

then the song, the cascading soprano waterfall

a river through canyon walls of operatic proportion

the song was right here

right here in the house

Chapter four

Electricity

After she fed the dogs and exited the kitchen she glanced

toward the ceiling   a tilted '50s light shade centering the wallboard

the nest!

the bird simply tweezered the whole production and moved it

from porch window to living room

the fire made in the antique Ashley stove warmed the whole

family   stock dogs   tiny brown speckled eggs   and woman

with long silver hair

Chapter five

Moon

She napped dreamily that afternoon as the sky darkened and the

wind sang through the canyons in ripeness

branches and leaves swayed a hula made from desert

rain forest in preparation for the deluge

it would not come till a moon slice past midnight and ferociously

ping the tin roof for an hour

ta-tamp tamp ta-tamp ta-tamp tamp ta-tamp

ta-tamp tamp

Chapter six

The End & Return

a virtually unstudied bird
—Tucson Audubon office

now the nest destroyed

like the year before and the year before

(the one inside the Weber grill lid outside)

dispersal   destruction   fury

other builders out there, other pairs, other pulsating lovers

ovum hardshell fusion chick

fledged

hopping the dance somewhere

moonwalking a tin roof   flying the world

Water Wonder

In Arizona summer clouds cover and soften the land and skin

a few drops   a few drops   while in North Dakota a two-pound hailstone

gets stored in a freezer for show

oceans lakes and rivers poisoned daily by war and transportation

mining   medicine   nuclear fission   and cow pies

what meaning does the dog find with her radar ears and laser nose (the one
who didn't get hit by the killer hail)

one more chew of green grass   one more drink from the creek

Chama

Up the brown curve of earth then a shift
to jagged ridge and downward into green river swirl

The majesty of red dirt and green water touch
her hands dipped from a crouch, the muscles in the
thighs taut and off balance feels good

icy green water from the red mountains promise more
green like verdolagas and alfalfa

good mammalian food and then a rise up, a standing
by the water that lifts up and up and up

a stream on consciousness, a light in surround

está bien

Fluorescence

Diamond dust over everything in night

in night within night, a rapture and the chill
of only seeing what you're allowed to see

a mighty systemic wave of energy
a gender dance and even a devouring

of light, brothers and sisters hunting for
the filament, the chain down the abandoned
railroad tracks

or through the mesquite bosque by the stock pond

I saw a single one two years in a row in the same place

Firefly

Conjuring

in the bear's shadow a leafing out
perhaps a thistle lavender and white

steep fall of the wind cuts by ears
and the bear stays, not judged

there was simply nobody home

in the sublethal theater of war and colony collapse
the poison was systemic   the leafing out tainted
only protected by prayer

and then some movement like the drum
of an ancient song

fear underfoot, nobody home, a light
brimming on the road of the bear.

Late Fall

Solitude is the deepest well I have ever come across.
—Roderick MacIver

the illumination pierced

first one leaf   then the next

yellow flame (circle broken)

the long arm of deadwood holds
            the bow   the arrow
            flicker stabs a green pecan
            ash tree creaking door hinge
            a mountain folds into the roof

            as I shovel back, shovel back
            like a dog drinking

(tiny opera of grief)

1.   Where did the love go after it rained down your thighs

        kept on raining past toes, grass roots and snails

        love that sparked key seeds on wind to make yellow pines
        and black, fir trees to golden spruce, oh where

        please forgive me my smallness, a little mouse who sings

2.   she had her heart out on a camping plate in the moonlight
        her head out in the hurricane of consciousness

        this was a scandal of love   hardscrabble yearning for kin

        like the day she found the canyon wren still gone dead on the hay bale

        one hay straw jet fast needle into the heart

San Juan's Day

She's been dreaming water into the earth for a week, brittle long days.

The dreaming hopeless.

Ground water nothing but vapor in air   soundless vapor.

She wished she could whistle and call forth more fumes
from the Oracle at Delphi
from Thunderbird
from hula dancers
from San Juan in all his baptismal rivers

The Doppler map seemed fitted for depression

  you couldn't dance to it and make it all happy and forthright in its predictions

couldn't bring it barley cakes or chant *Doppler Doppler Doppler . . . tell us*

a different truth about rain

She'll dream more water into the drying springs and into the saguaros who

bloomed this year in a fever

as if no rain were coming down to roots anytime soon
as if it were the very last bloom

How to feed a horse

It is different from feeding a growing boy
like James, who could eat a horse

still, I am enamored of horse eyelashes
and mules' and llamas' longer even

there is no shirking their loving glances
I'm being roped in, lassoed by lashes to
a feeding seduction, intimate sharing

so bring on the boxes of rinsed carrots
and let me splat a striped watermelon
on the ground

for I am satisfied by approximations
to the big fabled mouths, cartoon teeth
crunching   crunching

Little Sure Shot

Engrossed in Annie Oakley bio
I travel through chronology admiring
her kindness   philanthropy

all women should handle firearms
as well as they do babies
fifteen thousand women trained in Little Sure Shot's
classes over a lifetime

Bob the dog stomps and whisper barks

I look up, then down

the rattler has already passed

two feet ahead of my bare soles

three feet a-coming, slowly

not twelve inches away I startle

and jump over the crawling tail end

call the dogs and hustle inside

No scarier than Kaiser Wilhelm
holding cigarette in hand for
Annie's shot to blast tobacco through
the finite

NUMEROLOGY

One

A new year wintering home
imperceptibly turning south with
snow drifts from the Arctic

I have nothing and know nothing
but the slow growth in the garden
its promise of root vegetables and greens

some time ahead growth   expected

baits you into thinking   life is new

Two

in his hidden life the banker dealt
himself a card

Queen of Spades, no good

he dealt another, Three of Diamonds

in this game, Jacks are most valuable

so Queens and Threes might as well
be trying to cross the border to a new life

all the while knowing they are garbage

useless cards in the shuffling
looking for place
looking for worth

flat, edges ragged, but adding up to something with
the help of friends and other denominations

the Queens and the Threes line up
get processed and counted

are discarded once again.

Three

one coconut cocktail against three
green olives   quite a contest

not like the shake-a-shake of jowls
and hips under the summer hose

the Wilderness Society banned skepticism
demanded serenity and whistling
(the chapter in Nova Scotia dropped out)

there is so much floating crap in the oceans
will the waves reflect the sun?

someone indicated sublime beings
sitting under an umbrella, two shake-jowled
dogs at their feet

perhaps they'd come to ban malls the size
of football fields, perhaps
they'd come to do some archeology

Four

I am leached of meaning and crave
that salted plot of curiosity
o green, I love you green, sang Lorca
seeds of belief greening the night in its bright abyss

the words *pasture, catkin,* and *lark* have been
dropped from the Oxford Children's Dictionary
replaced by *hard drive, software* and *platform*
the better to virtually camp anywhere

some kind of modern bloodletting, indeed an
application of leeches to the subatomic layer of
energy and mass

Five

for Donna

She calls at 6:30 a.m. to announce she's being served a breve.
later,   corn   greens   red potatoes   and squash from the garden
alongside fried cod

I wish I could send you dear sister, my expensive cotton sheets
but your marriage bed requires California King

I sleep with the Queens, so that won't do

why one should feel so royal when claimed by cancer
suddenly the world realizes your only precious life
the path you carved and the people you nourished
the endless work of attention

your always, sometimes hiding, love

Six

Trumpets of obstruction march through Congress
flat on its back like a cockroach.

Everyday's paper and glassed news scrolls mind
poison and dung, the misuse of thinking squandered
on power duels and jockeying (forgive me horses)
for center widescreen.

no matter the lie, the lie.

The challenging riddle is about solvency and heart.
Billion dollar numbers are spread by priority and put
before every intelligence
because, so much depends on calming it all down.

Seven

for Barrie

The Great Transition

occurred when atoms became so curious they wondered:

what is infinity?

is it like reverie or wheat-colored prairies blue ocean prairies

watering sea life

does it hum like the dinosaurs savoring their bigness

or speak silence fluently like Pablo Neruda?

no complacent cartoons, the atoms, good meditators all

there was nothing left but transit, and more transit and more

Eight

Meditation in, for, and by shopping.
meditation during recess with crows cawing
meditation of the heart and out through arteries
forest meditation, branches latched and singing

oh the leaves   oh the leaves

the meditation of the dinner bell and the scarf
and even that nonlethal one with the revolver
refrigerator mantra like electric ice cubes
repetitive sounds clutch and shifter of the mind
sitting in loving kindness annihilates death now
and prayer not enough though it works, close to
the heart of great

Nine

How the skin holds Larcena Pennington
and a will to move finds 1800s
Arizona history on the second
page of the *Daily Star*

the will to move bodily after Apaches
attacked   deep spear wounds in the back
how to be white and traveling West
a woman
how to be a white woman
thrown for dead under the mesquite
down canyon

no clothes but torn bloody slip final
rescue only through the will to

move inch by inch

how to be a white woman married along
Sonoita Creek
was a privilege.

Ten

The missing photo   a distant traveler on unfamiliar ground
the airplane lost to radar
a girl stolen from her bed
a blind dog sensing caravan   the Saharan caravan walking
camels to salt
nomadic route now lost to trucks
a missing photo
the silent songs   no laughter no

Eleven

retina of a dying world
how does it return to what it saw
open or closed

a rolling restless seeing sometimes
urgent   fronting the cranial bone
just so, at rest

Spanish sounds a secret charm for wisdom
like that cliche "on the horizon"

vision, the iris, your lids wide open
standing barefoot

you long for love and how to get there
eyeballs on the dying world

Twelve

wake up rock   said the blade of grass pressing

wake up wound   said the surgeon

wake up tenant   said the robber

and wake up mouth said the expletive: even two lips cannot
                            equal one word

wake up success   said perseverance: be tolerant, don't growl and be patient

wake up sleeper   said the dream: the earth is spinning mightily at its
                        core   your magnetism spills out into the day

wake up pilgrim   said the sun: I am already shining on your navel

Thirteen

(Remembering Federico Garcia Lorca)

The child poet draws an A, a mountain with a cross-stroke

over and over the A's, the mountains cut in middle.

The letters work their way into the hand with practice

no rain nor twine can place them there.

The poet draws and draws off the darkside of the planet

off abuela, her name the ah-nouncement of A,

Off the sound, child formulates sight and sign

a linkage between two temples.

All breath and mystery combined here

move the hand to be.

Fourteen

I know before he does.

The sky will light up with sparkling chrysanthemums red
green silver heaven bombs followed by oohs and aahs

Who thought of the dogs in 1776?

Were they paraded in tricorner hats and patriotic bows or
left to run out to the endless spaces
wheat fields and corn sparkling rivers lakes small streams
with silver-lined fish   bordered by tall maples

or to burrow into the hay mow, dig under the leaf litter
hide under the pigeon hutches?

No safety there now. The open fields and streams gone
fish poisoned maples stripping down to barren

The war that comes on the Fourth of July shakes Jack the dog's ribs
and pierces the eardrums beyond any rhythm imaginable
marking the national boundaries of country and Earth

Fifteen

1

When you speak to me about your favorite jar or
the new recipe you made for Hound Cake

I wonder about the rigor of words
how they dissipate, fall flat as an iron on a shirt
get used as the shield:

no one will ever share my bed again

2

Tonight I smoke the letters out they
curl   overlap   aggregate   arise as mist and fume
indecipherable   addicting

Kenneth Koch wonders if poems are psychodegradable

St. Theresa declares words prepare the soul and make it ready
for tenderness

Sixteen

When gray is so kind to you blue just won't do
blue of the heart inking out word webs, drama and
reckoning

a pulse lettered freely, no signet ring stamp or green
marble in hand

my heart, my life, a quickening in spring and fair waters
tighten down the tremors

all energy blue-ing out to red through oxygen

all energy filled with you, darling, arisen

may desire always overflow your daily need

HER(E)

Now 70

for Barbara Babcock
"betwixt and between"

The birthday an island of air and dirt
no longer ocean or very lake of the heart

a whole breathing under the belly of her mother
now surfaces and gulps sound

What world opens with a slap
head no longer rotating effortlessly in
the Oceania of quickening

now upside down, now resting on the breast
of earth

now knowing
this is the land of in between
flesh and spirit rocking hard
teeth grabbing life until they fall out

journey looking for the carnal door to weightlessness again

Sophie

fool, it's simply an absence of genetics

not bad luck that

slights and slopes brain waves of language   emotion

across the autistic spectrum

"I closed my eyes and everything was fire"

then I opened them in German class and could not sit another moment

chemical saturation or electrical expansion

a gleaning or a planting in neat deficient rows

crazy mindfulness, just so

ten years younger in social maturation

she speaks to your youth and performs TV immersion

each plot detail her personal sword

what is autism but a new bird in the nest we

identify or not

Immigrants

Her given name had something to do with a blue scarf
and hundreds of species

his name, peeling and sealing on a crackled sign
call it grassy   shiny residue   time scrabble

you could identify both with binoculars

top of head red, a native ginger, frontal protrusions, female
top of head shaved, extra tall, frontal protrusion, male
                a Caucasian rambler within range

they were not a pair but comingled regularly to
take away the sadness of their species

in Spring, the two would wilt and stutter
first in Spanish, then English

then break out in song
the bilingual way

Etymology Tree

Rita brings streamers of life into the room
wisdom words, smiles and
the allure of life-changing vacations.

The vacation word means to empty completely
and thus I think I'll take a trip to Pipevine Swallowtail Ranch

where the horses admire lupines
and the moles play dodgeball under the earth.

I've heard about this place and if I drive carefully enough
with big tires cushioning the road rough,
my intentions might arrive safely too.

Vacation,

a good word rooted like a tree that says

you can do it, you can go there,
and kneel down low

to blow American oppression off your back
maybe lay down with ear to ground
and see if you can find the ball

make it move somewhere
make it move.

Royal Whim

Crabapples and common vipers gathered around All Fools' Day, a day not

determined by weather or calendar, but by Queen May herself

She was a working angel in queenly form and did not announce destination or arrival

A suitcase at the side porch door signalled her trips and travails, and the crown

she fashioned of rosemary and marigolds proclaimed: *Mary Mary Mary May,*

you smell yellow, you smell gay

The Mary Crown pushed her forward and out of the floral openings toward a

buzzy future of fools garbed and floundering for the Spring Reckoning

She appeared instantaneously in a diaphanous gown:

This is Last Call she chirped

All the grassy fools on Fools' Day Noon took off with the Queen, took off amongst the

flowers blowing toward the west

Translation

Why does she despair when the clutches of quail appear in their season

parents scurrying a dozen tiny entities on feet across the road

is it fair to despair in the air of bright existence, that same sun demanding

we take charge of our planetary planning

with boast or grief, sigh, hunched shoulders, a dark-spun silver thread of

sorrow has sewn her pocket shut

there is no reason to be optimist when pulling the Ace of Cups overflowing

in abundance and liquid heart

for on this day of high sun and quail song, those clicks and wails, those

bubbling bird murmurs that seem to say "get along, get along"

she sinks to the timbre of that cruel universal language called Black

How to repair with eyes complex enough
they know in all directions

see colors unknown to dogs and grandfathers

how to repair and recall the name for things like muscle and greenery

the feeling that goes with awareness of ants

how we can't know the heartbeats of bats, so black they are blue

the self split   two trains passing   how to repair with the big eye

worn words that have come the whole way

what force could interrupt hibernation proper   a gleaming sword pointed at the

molten core

caves and burrows rock canopies reflecting downwind cold

carving of last name that marks stable and recognized   carving that doesn't

know where to find food in winter

Solution

Ann thought the problem in
not out
a layer of electricity bonding tissue to bone
would well the whole body up with glistening

the better to see the ghosts who'd just arrived
the better to touch them and wonder about the silence

it was glistening too and you could hear a high hum
cushioning the air

they were all seated together in the ghostly night
feeling exaltation, feeling the problem in

Elder

cracking the language alive with memory holes

she searches for the right words   the locations proper

names   nouns

all the knowns nounzy fever   a dead drop of forgetfulness

salt and straight vinegar of age

Story

I
Amazon,
fierce river so dangerous the Spanish merged
your frothing with women warriors

take note travelers: the way is dangerous
                    for the way is open

an open garrulous mouth, drooling
                    of resource extraction
                    and people destruction

oh those blue macaws shrieking in flight hundreds of them
crying out over the howler monkeys atop the canopy—where do you go?

II

No noisier place this rain forest, with eerie hissings, buzzflashes and breadfruit
falling from on high. Sounds vibrant, shocking, spectacular

III

but nothing compared to the fall of a giant ceiba tree after the high pitched
careening of a chainsaw has cut through the heart
nothing

a universe cut down, the stories invented to explain it:

giant tree gave birth to the Amazon River
the river gave birth to the Amazon Peoples
the insects traveling its bark and spine
gave birth to all the colors of the peoples of the rain forest

                    * (III) Kayapo tribal story from the Northwest Amazon

Ambush

Her mind immersed in the hidden   a stalled bloom or
disappearing orchid   reminded of unknowing

even as she attuned to seeing

no clock or card sign defined outcome nor thermostatic balance
nor hat hung securely on the rack

the day was done and day again made its own drought like
starving angry fly who remembers red juice

Gender-flipping on Pancake Day (Shrove Tuesday)

Who goes first in the pancake throw? shouts the Irish baker shriving with

wheat, syrup and artful flipping

Rose advances dressed in houndstooth suit and black paddy cap, picks

from the stack of medium doilies with crisp butter edges and starts sailing

them   high   high   high

to add to the chaff, dross, pencil rubbings, to the wastelands large

as cities, those germinating barges fat with garbage and plastic, to fatness!

omelets fried in salt butter, the twelve-egg cake with two cups of cream

to equal sugar

in the warm suit Rose could bulge at the waist, still look stately when she

puffs her cigar in the face of the shriver. It was Tuesday, and for forty days

and nights she would flip and wander like a passion flower vining through

Spring complete whether dressed or not

Guidebook to the Maladies

It's true, the mates, whether homebound or sailing, would often presuppose their relationship as enemy territory, the war of process, a mutual victimization. Mate One was often ravaged by superstition and would make Mate Two stop the car at Apache Junction while on the road. Here, at the little commune called Four Drag Ranch, instant ritual could be had for a box of raisins, a bag of popcorn. The mate soldiers particularly enjoyed grate-sitting al fresco—the geometric patterns left on their butts after a twenty-minute meditation caused pain and delight, a tinge of agony, pierce of joy, like a paper cut on the lip. "I can't believe how cleansed I feel, my hiney transformed into a flesh waffle." "Yes, yes, mate, I concur . . . it's as if my heart were drenched by a twelve-inch rain, and then dried and pampered with duckling-soft towels."

For Barbara Allen

No content   no context   just a girl leaning into the road on a

bicycle. She left the good dogs at home out of the heat, sunshine
on the road, little rocks staying away from her tires out of appreciation
for shamanic pedaling, no journey happening, no context, sweet
swishing songs of the creosote and a quick salute to the grand
saguaro thinking about blooming.

Bicycle seat getting hard but feet still happy, the wind billows her
shirt like a white sail and she rings the bell when the quail skitter ahead.
She feels her heart shining heart shining and knows the real goodness
of spoked wheels and strong legs, she knows the goodness of the wind
and the sound of tires tiring along.

Red Juice

The Secret Twilight Society meets under the pomegranate tree
as long as secrets can live. In summer, when the cicadas drone their hissing
heat, and more children are apt to invade the pomegranate zone, the two
major secret girls invent a code word: F-111. They are Tucson natives, know
the neighborhood from stink bugs and fig eaters to Mrs. Carlson's trash; they
know their code word is also the audible sign of a swept wing zeroing to
touchdown at the Air Force base. Secret Girl One signals Two by plugging
her ears and looking skyward; Two responds knowingly by turning her back
after a pause and spitting on the ground.

"Do you know what I love, secret girl?"

Closure

Mending a zipper to only partially zip for the rest of its life, she wondered
how many

       cracks   riffs   separations   could be treated so

just leave part out: a zipper coil, two stitches, the jag of the flesh cut you snip

or, erasing footsteps in the washbed
a tire track in the snow

how many stifled words eaten, eaten alive for sure

how what's gone missing   how what's hidden

performs a new repair

Even grief gets hungry and demands more grief.

    —Joy Harjo

In the darkest passage of the holy book there was no sound or word, you could
not take it by mouth

one would need to feed the nervous system some other way, not by mouth

one would need to lay prostrate on the ground with one's eyes and mouth closed
hands stretched forward   laid out bare in the night's imaginings   the dark

like the ground needed bodies close and alive   not the bones marked by
centuries of stones   everlasting

prone on the ground an event of sincere gratitude   nostrils breathing life force
and dirt

upside down world to the woman standing on the tarmac, her coat blowing wide
open in the wind

Defining the Rules

more or less anthem

plus thicker than night music

we wondered if soul was off-color

or drought-stricken or glittering

most mad and moonly e.e. day

most sane and sunly Corpus Christi

visions secret forty years of cloister

but sane and sunly e. e. day

feast, oh feast feasts, sisters of the blood

we must chant more and unchant less

recluse and wonder, our living bread

on tongues of song, slangy

Transfiguration

How much does the tree remain in this
paper, its bark   nesting places   the branch arms
and seasonal change?

how much mother's milk remains in our bodies alongside
the loving rainbow chain of parental DNA

or when does the bud in its flowering pass over
into enchantment
and then turn downward into dry end times

or the water evaporating and receding, atonement for
our human firing up of energy

                  oh water, how will the tides turn?

Last night when the full moon chased me from window
to window its startled face shining on my attention

I asked it about the water, the tides

I asked it about the trees that transcribed this poem

Would a prophet undo clutter in the writing?

endless pumping of words, breast milk for infancy in liquid

drinkable form, a purpose to propel

the goat herder and healer told clan Little Dog the truths about

talking fire, that back end of language generating syllables and

consolation pronsolation dawnsolation energy

how getting there required the goodness road through chaos and

out again along the wooded hillsides, goat friends surrounding

but where to in the words words not needing readers
where to the solation of sound sense

aspirations are but air fulfilled by hope in alphabets dreams and

animal talk all cluttered together in song

Biographical Note

Janice Dewey's career in literature and teaching began at a young age with scholarships to live and study in both Argentina (American Field Service) and Chile (Fulbright). She interviewed and published about Jorge Luis Borges and shook Pablo Neruda's hand after one of his readings in Santiago.

She has taught Spanish, women's studies, humanities, and contemporary poetry at the University of Arizona and its Poetry Center for decades and made the documentary video *Waist-High in the World* about disability writer Nancy Mairs, which is available on YouTube. This is her first book at age seventy-three.